PRODUCTIVE PLANNING

PRODUCTIVE PLANNING

How To Get More Done

James R Sherman

KOGAN
PAGE

First published in the United States of America in 1991 by Crisp Publications Inc, 95 First Street, Los Altos, California 94022, USA.

This edition first published in Great Britain in 1991 by Kogan Page Ltd, 120 Pentonville Road, London N1 9JN.

British Library Cataloguing in Publication Data

A CIP record for this book is available from the British Library.

ISBN 0–7494–0585–6

Printed and bound in Great Britain by
Biddles Ltd, Guildford and Kings Lynn

Contents

About This Book

Productive Planning is not like most books. It stands out from other self-help books in an important way. It's not a book to read – it's a book to *use*. The unique format of this book and the many case studies and worksheets encourage the reader to get involved and try some new ideas immediately.

The simple yet sound concepts and techniques presented will help readers to understand the benefits that come with planning and will help them learn to take action on their plans in order to become more successful both in their careers and personal lives.

Productive Planning (and other titles in this series) can be used effectively in a number of ways. Here are some possibilities:

- *Individual study*. Because the book is self-instructional, all that is needed is a quiet place, some time and a pencil. By completing the activities and exercises, the reader will not only get valuable feedback, but also practical ideas for self-improvement.

- *Workshops and seminars*. The book is ideal for assigned reading prior to a workshop or seminar. With the basics in hand, the quality of the participation will improve, and more time can be spent on concept extensions and applications during the programme. The book is also effective when it is distributed at the beginning of a session, and participants work through the contents.

- *Open learning*. Books can be sent to those unable to attend head office training sessions.

This book can be used in a variety of learning situations depending on the objectives, programme or ideas of the user.

One thing is certain: even after it has been read, this book will be looked at – and thought about – again and again.

CHAPTER 1

Introduction to Planning

Welcome to *Productive Planning*. This book will provide some simple and easily followed techniques that will pay you personal dividends. The results you can get from faithfully applying the techniques presented can be dramatic! Hard to believe? Take the plunge and see for yourself.

'A journey of a thousand miles begins with a single step.'

You can be sure that when Lao Tzu, the sixth-century Chinese philosopher, wrote that phrase he didn't just vault over the top of the Great Wall and take off. People travelling a thousand miles – or one mile – should have some idea of where they're going when that first step is taken. Otherwise they'll end up like Alice in Wonderland.

> 'Cheshire-Puss', [. . . said Alice] 'Would you tell me, please, which way I ought to go from here?'
> 'That depends a good deal on where you want to get to', said the Cat.
> 'I don't much care where —' said Alice.
> 'Then it doesn't matter which way you go', said the Cat.
> '— so long as I get *somewhere*', Alice added as an explanation.
> 'Oh, you're sure to do that', said the Cat, 'if you only walk long enough.'

Alice obviously doesn't know where she's going and doesn't seem too concerned about it. Some people are like that. But a lot more people get frustrated when they can't find their way to a promising future. These disappointed men and women want to get ahead in life, and they want to climb the ladder of success, but they can't even find the ladder.

They try to do all the things that 'successful' people do. They go to workshops, retreats and seminars to learn how to feel better about themselves. They read all the motivational material they can get their hands on. Sometimes they can even *see* themselves skipping down the yellow brick road to a happy and prosperous future, but that's as far as they get. Most of them are just plain dead in the water.

Their expectations of success usually last a week or so, and then they find themselves back in the same old rut of not knowing what to do next. They want to get better at what they're doing, but they just don't know how – or where – to start. They don't have a plan, and they don't know how to produce one. Many of them feel lost and adrift on the tide of humanity.

You know how frustrating it can be, or you wouldn't be reading this book.

How do you feel?

Do you know where you're going, or are you just plodding along like Alice? Do you want something better than what you have now? Do you want to turn your hopes and dreams into reality? Are you trying to get from point A, where you are now, to point B, where you want to be tomorrow?

Write your point A and point B in the space below.

POINT A: Where I am now:

_____

POINT B: Where I want to be some time in the future:

_____

You and I both know that you can satisfy your desires if you can only get your hands on the right tools. All it takes is *planning*, and that's what this book is going to teach you to do.

> **WARNING.** If you're already completely satisfied with your current level of productivity and think planning is a waste of time, then go no further. This book is *not* for you.

You can start your journey towards a successful future by taking a close look at the definition of planning.

A definition of planning

Planning is the design of a hoped-for future and the development of effective steps for bringing it about.

- It's a rational, systematic method of *decision-making* and *problem-solving*.

- It combines your experience, knowledge and skill with *realistic assessments* of where you are and where you'd like to be.

- It points out the *risks* you face in charting a course into an unknown future.

- It helps you to identify the *hazards* and *opportunities* that can determine your chances of success.

- It shows you how to turn opportunities into attainable *goals* within specified periods of time.

- It helps you to reach critical *milestones* on the road to success.

- It makes you think of your future in terms of *facts* instead of *fantasies*.

- It gives you the *power* you need to control your future.

Planning takes what you know about where you are now, flavours it with what you'd like to be in the future, mixes in a liberal dash of your experience, knowledge and skill, and gives you a mulligan stew of successful outcomes.

Planning paves the way for a future in which you become the kind of person you really want to be.

What is this thing called planning?

Planning . . .

. . . is *open-minded* and *flexible*.

. . . encourages *change* and *modification*.

. . . clarifies your *image of reality*, enhances your *visions of the future* and

. . . gauges your *chances of success* by telling you how far and how fast you need to go to reach a goal you really want.

Major types of planning

There are four major types of planning. One focuses on the future, another looks at the here-and-now. Two more deal with the way planning is done.

1. Type A planning

If you're getting geared up for events that haven't happened yet, such as:

> getting a new job;
> awaiting the arrival of a baby;
> avoiding a serious illness; or
> preparing for a change in the weather,

you're involved in *future planning*. You can't control these impending events, but you can be ready for them when they pay you a visit.

2. Type B planning

You're involved in *here-and-now planning* if you're trying hard to change your present behaviour by:

staying on a diet;
breaking a bad habit;
taking a much-needed holiday; or
starting a new relationship.

You can control these events and effect the change you want in the future by taking action today.

3. Type C planning

If you're trying to get where you want to go by taking your lead from what others have done in the past, you're involved in *follow-the-leader planning*.

And finally . . .

4. Type D planning

If you study a problem, check out alternative courses of action and select what you think is the most promising solution, then you're involved in *analytical planning*.

Now you're really getting into the thick of it. The following are some additional planning concepts.

The two planning models

Planning models are miniature representations of what goes on in the real world. They give you a mind's-eye view of what the planning process is all about.

Planning models provide the framework around which you can build any plan, no matter how complicated or long-lasting it might be. It can be a large corporate plan or a simple day-to-day plan for satisfying personal goals. Once you get accustomed to a planning framework, you can apply the model to anything.

The inside-out planning model

- It's based on you as a *unique individual*.

- It's tailored to what you're doing *now* and what you think you will be able to do in the *future*.

- It teaches you to concentrate on things you're *good at* and *enjoy doing*.

- It encourages you to do what's *possible*, instead of taking chances on hypothetical estimates of the world around you.

- It lets you work out what you *personally* need to do to reach your short-range and long-term goals.

- It calls for a lot of *self-appraisal*, which makes the process more reliable, because the qualities that describe you as an individual are more substantial and last longer than the qualities that describe the world you live in.

The outside-in planning model
- The primary focus of the outside-in model is on the people and events that exist in the world around you. You come *second*.

- It makes use of what *other people* think is happening now or is going to happen in the future.

- It calls for a continuous analysis of *outside* trends, conditions and other environmental factors.

- It causes *time lags* because it can only make use of information that other people have accumulated and are willing to provide to you.

Which model are they using?
Here are some examples of the two types of planning. For each one, decide which planning model is being used. Tick the appropriate box.

Slo Gro Company waits to hear the latest wide-scale economic forecasts before making a new investment. Inside-out ☐ Outside-in ☐

Rapidity Ltd always acts on the basis of what its managers already know about their own economic situation. Inside-out ☐ Outside-in ☐

John Cautious is waiting to buy a house until someone else tells him it's a buyer's market. Inside-out ☐ Outside-in ☐

Mary Ponder is waiting until she can get access to the information she needs before deciding what steps to take. Inside-out ☐ Outside-in ☐

Answers: Rapidity Ltd does inside-out planning. The others do outside-in planning. They also do a lot of waiting.

You've probably already guessed it. Everything you find in this book is geared toward the *inside-out planning model*.

The eight basic steps

The entire planning process can be summarised in these eight important steps.

1. Assessment
- You get an uneasy feeling about who you are and what you're doing.

- You decide you want to do better than you're doing now.

- You see where you are in life and recognise a need – as well as a desire – to change.

2. Commitment
- You make up your mind that you're going to change and you set your sights on doing something about it.

3. Investigation
- You collect data about yourself and the world in which you live.

- You study every aspect of your life, especially your history of successes and failures.

- You make a list of the skills you have to offer and the handicaps you have to bear.

- You examine the personal relationships you've had, especially those in which you've had to compete against others to get ahead.

- You work out how much time you're going to have available for trial and error.

- You identify the risks you will have to take to bring about the change you want.

4. Decision
- You get a premonition of what you think is going to happen.

- You apply your intuition to everything you learned in your investigation and then work out a list of alternative choices of what you want to do and when you want to do it.

5. Organisation
- You select the goals that are best suited to your needs.

- You choose a planning strategy that will do the best job of getting you where you want to go.

- You set priorities, establish timetables and work out how you're going to evaluate your progress.

- You choose a definite course of action.

6. Preparation
- You gather up everything you need to carry out your plan of action, including everything you read in this book.

- You fine-tune your plan and get ready to deal with any unforeseen circumstances.

7. Implementation
- You carry out a series of well-defined tasks, being sure to pause from time to time to see how well your performance is measuring up against your original expectations.

- You stop whenever you run into a problem. Then you quickly change direction and develop alternative ways of reaching your goal in the most effective manner.

8. Achievement
- You achieve your current goal and then start the process anew as you continue your climb up the ladder of success.

Is it all worth it? You bet it is!
Here's proof that planning works. Back in the 1950s, a behavioural research team from the Harvard Business School took a random sample of 100 members of the senior class and asked them what they would like to be doing ten years from graduation. All 100 said they would like to be wealthy, successful and significant forces in the business world.

The researches noted that of the 100 seniors, only ten had drawn up specific goals and put them in writing.

Ten years later, the research team paid a follow-up visit to the 100 subjects. They found that the ten graduates who had written down their goals *owned 96 per cent of the total wealth* of the 100-student sample.

Planning *does* pay off.

The benefits of planning

Planning can benefit you in so many ways it's hard to mention them all. Here are some benefits that stand out above the rest.

1. *Gives direction*: Planning stimulates you to think about the promise of the future rather than the failures of the past.

2. *Coordinates*: Planning ties all your efforts and aspirations together in a simple, easily understood, well-balanced programme.

3. *Provides standards*: Planning helps you to size up your

performance, measure your progress, and work out how well you're doing.

4. *Clarifies*: Planning helps you to work out what you really want out of life by cutting through all the superfluities that clutter up your mind.

5. *Prepares*: Planning gives you the tools you need to deal with sudden and unexpected problems that can hit you at any time and from any position.

6. *Reveals*: Planning gives you a clear picture of how different tasks and activities interact to ensure success in your overall quest.

7. *Stimulates*: Planning leads you onwards and upwards by providing the stimulation you need to avoid dead-ends and blind alleys in your work, creativity and personal relationships.

Planning improves your morale, your attitudes and your relationships with other people while giving you a sense of security about the days ahead.

The benefits sound almost too good to be true. But once you start to plan, you'll find that it's everything it's cracked up to be. It's a potent remedy for many of life's ills. There are, however, some pitfalls you should watch out for.

Dangers in planning

No process is foolproof, even when you think you've done everything right. Fortunately, none of the following dangers is so serious that you can't cut it down whenever it shows its ugly head.

1. Loss of spontaneity
Spontaneity comes with flexibility. It means taking advantage of spur-of-the-moment opportunities as soon as they happen. You can't plan to be spontaneous – that's a contradiction in terms. But you can plan to be flexible, and that's the key.

If your planning strategies are flexible, you'll gain spontaneity, encounter a wealth of opportunities, and have an open road in your drive to success.

2. Too much faith in the process
If you put too much faith in how you're going to carry out your plans, you may be afraid to break out and try something new. Your singlemindedness will keep you from seeing obstacles and alternatives that could affect your chances of success. Instead of moving ahead, you'll pull up short and your plans will come to a grinding halt.

3. Lack of growth
If you don't grow, you'll stagnate and never get off square one. In order to grow, you need the excitement and stimulation of new ideas, new knowledge and new methods. So no matter how good you think your plans are when you first start out, you still have to allow for modification and improvement along the way as new concepts germinate and begin to bear fruit.

4. Psychological distress
Undisciplined planning can lead to shortsightedness, a lack of creativity and an inability to innovate. That can leave you as frustrated and unhappy as having no plans at all. Disciplined planning can remove the stress and make your journey a pleasant one.

5. Over-reliance on methods
If *how* it's done becomes more important than *whether* it's done, then methods, techniques and procedures will gradually take over the entire goal-seeking process, and your dreams for the future will fade like a summer romance.

The benefits in planning, as you can see, still far outweigh the dangers. You can avoid these and other dangers entirely by keeping an open mind and not allowing yourself to become addicted to the process.

You have started to build your future

You have already taken two very significant steps towards a confident future.

1. You have *recognised* the *need* to plan your future.
2. You have *committed* yourself to being involved with the process of planning.

Lots of people never get as far as you are right now, so you're already ahead of the rest. Chapter 2 looks at some of the reasons why many of your colleagues and competitors will never catch up.

CHAPTER 2
Why People Don't Plan

Planning takes lots of concentrated thought. You have to know where you are in life, what options are open to you, where you want to go, and what you have to do to get there. That requires self-examination and a thorough analysis of your strengths, weaknesses, philosophy and attitudes.

The element of chance

Chance is the impersonal, purposeless determiner of unaccountable happenings. It's pure chance when a coconut falls out of a palm tree and lands unnoticed in the sand. But if the coconut were to land on your head, you'd consider that bad luck, and you'd be right.

Good luck is simply chance that benefits human beings. You can't influence chance, but you can control the way you respond to it. If no one was around to see or hear the coconut fall, it would merely be a chance occurrence. But if you saw the coconut fall and jumped out of the way to avoid it, you could say you were lucky, and you'd be right again.

The planning process shapes your luck by showing you how to respond to falling coconuts and other external chances of life. You can, through careful planning, improve your potential for good luck and enhance your chance of success by recognising good fortune whenever it occurs and by applying yourself to the opportunities it presents. If you don't respond to chance in a predetermined fashion, you run the risk of having bad luck or no luck at all.

Maybe the thought of all those mental aerobics is what makes some people *players* instead of planners. You've probably run into some of these players from time to time and heard their comments about planning.

Players think it's a waste of time to try to affect what's going to happen in a distant, hazy future. They would rather rely on the mysteries of chance to bring them happiness and prosperity. But what they don't know is that no one who has relied on chance alone has ever been consistently successful.

Just what effect does chance have on your life? It can affect you a lot, or it can pass you by entirely.

People who rely *entirely* on chance events for their success always seem to fall short. And it isn't only their response to the whims of Mother Nature that clouds their future. Much of their misfortune lies in their dogged determination not to plan. Following are some of the major reasons why they choose to go this route.

Negative attitudes
If you turned on your tape recorder, you'd probably pick up comments like these when the subject of planning came around.

☐ 'Planning is too time consuming. I've got better things to do.'

☐ 'There's too much work involved in planning. It's not worth the effort.'

☐ 'The future is too unpredictable for planning to have any value. You can't see into the future, so why try to plan for it?'

☐ 'I don't understand the planning process, and I won't waste my time trying to learn something I don't understand.'

☐ 'We should live for today and not think about the future. What's happening now is more important than what might happen tomorrow.'

☐ 'People should live by intuition and not by planning. I've got a gut feeling that what I'm doing is all right, and that takes care of all my planning needs.'

_____

_____

_____

Does any of that sound familiar? Have *you* ever said any of those things? Go back and tick the ones you've said, or might say. Add any similar comments that occur to you.

Maybe you can also identify with one or more of the players described below. Please write your answers in the spaces provided.

Stubbornness

Stubbornness in the face of conflicting evidence almost always guarantees failure. It's one of Arnold's major weaknesses, and it usually shows up when he's drawn into the planning process against his will. He resents having to plan because someone told him to. On many occasions he has deliberately set out to sabotage the planning process as a singleminded way of asserting his individuality. It also gives him a means of avoiding responsibility if the planning process ever falls short of expectations.

Have you ever deliberately resisted someone else's efforts to get you to plan something? Describe what you did.

_____

_____

_____

Do you know why you did it? _____

_____

Excessive optimism

Carlotta is a dyed-in-the-wool optimist who sees no reason to plan because she just knows the future is going to be every bit as rosy as the present. She ignores threats, discards bad news when she hears it, and refuses to deal with obstacles that are staring her in the face. Her excessive zeal, need for immediate gratification and inability to distinguish reality from fantasy mislead her into believing that life is always going to be a bed of roses.

This blissful dreamer lacks the foresight she needs to adjust to sudden and unexpected problems. She has not disciplined herself to plan ahead, so she's generally unable to respond when her house of cards comes tumbling down.

What feelings do *you* have about the future that you think might justify your reasons for not planning?

_____

_____

_____

Lack of perception

Dale has no notion of where he is in life, where he wants to go, or what he has to do to be successful. He doesn't know his own strengths and weaknesses, and he can't see the obstacles and hazards that threaten his growth and development. He can't begin the planning process because he can't see what he has to do to get off dead centre.

Sometimes Dale divides his world into such small segments that he loses all perspective about what's going on around him. He interprets current events according to his own biased notions because he can't make head or tail of what other people have told him. He's left with pieces of a puzzle that he can't put back together. He goes through life eliminating all kinds of planning options that might otherwise lead to successful outcomes.

People like Dale are so saturated with random information, and so confused about what they're trying to do, that they fail to see the changes that are happening all about them. When they finally see where they are in life, they're too mixed up to shift gears or start again with long-range plans.

What do you see as the most confusing set of circumstances you have to deal with, and how is it holding you back?

_____

_____

_____

_____

_____

_____

Intellectual and communication problems

Susan doesn't plan because she can't muster the knowledge and skill that's needed to chart a course from the present to the future. She has a hard time identifying obstacles, and when she finally stumbles into one, she has difficulty getting round it before it starts causing problems.

Susan has never learned the basic elements of planning, so she doesn't have the tools she needs to be able to identify problems or express them in ways that would lead to workable solutions.

It's like not realising that her house is on fire, in spite of the smoke that fills the room. And even when she recognises that she's in danger, she still doesn't know how to call for help.

Have you ever had a situation where you were in over your head and didn't know how to get out of it? Describe the situation.

_____

_____

_____

Would planning have helped? How? _____

_____

Inflexibility

Bob not only ignores the benefits of planning, he also turns his back on the knowledge that other people have gained from the planning process. And because he has insulated himself from the advice, suggestions and counsel of people who have shared positive experiences through planning, his hopes for success have generally fallen short.

Bob can never know and understand every detail that might affect him in the future. The world is just too complex. The best he can do is to try to absorb, understand and apply as much as he can through the planning process. But as long as he chooses an inflexible course that ignores the experience of people who have gone before him, he has no one to blame but himself for his lack of growth and development.

Admit it, you thought your mother was wrong about the need to plan, so you went ahead and did it your own way. What happened when you ignored advice?

_____

_____

Problems with urgency

A fundamental principle of successful planning is to give highest priority to tasks that have the greatest importance. Greta doesn't do that. She sets her priorities (if you can call them that) according to how urgent her tasks are instead of how important they are. She never plans ahead, because she's too busy putting out fires. She's so wrapped up in trying to solve short-term crises that she seldom gets a chance to work on things that have long-term implications. And it's usually the urgent need of someone else that seems to get most of Greta's attention.

The only way Greta is going to reach her hoped-for levels of success is by establishing a plan that allows her to reach her own aspirations first and still have time to deal with the urgent needs of others as time permits.

Have you ever felt compelled to take care of someone else's problems while your own remained unattended to? What were the consequences?

_____

_____

_____

Social taboos and environmental blocks

Social taboos keep Ralph from walking round in his underwear in a heat wave. Environmental blocks keep him from taking advantage of opportunities that exist outside his own restricted life space. He's afraid of venturing into different environments, whether in small towns, big cities, little companies, large corporations or foreign countries.

Traditions, social customs and regional folklore often keep Ralph from adapting to the changing nature of the world around him. He can't plan for the future because he's unable – or unwilling – to adapt to new surroundings or to accept new standards of behaviour. He often responds to new cultures or environments by saying, 'That's not the way I do things', or 'That's not the way I've been brought up.'

Can you remember any times when you refused to act because some deep-seated habit, social custom, precept or folklore prevented you from doing so?

_____

_____

_____

Limited viewpoints

Tina doesn't plan because she doesn't like to try new, untested methods or venture into unfamiliar territory. She prefers to live in the present, doing what she's always done and is most comfortable with. She's ready and willing to judge new ideas, but not to generate them. She sometimes senses a need to change, but she'll usually back away from doing anything about it if she thinks she might run into problems. She doesn't know what her strengths and weaknesses are because she's never been tested against real adversity. Her past successes have been in recognisable situations where she's been able to apply familiar strategies.

Tina is going to have to venture beyond her limited horizon if her hopes for success are to be fulfilled. Otherwise she'll spend most of her time bathed in mediocrity.

What basic ethical, religious, social, political or other ideas do you subscribe to that you think might be keeping you from getting ahead in life?

_____

_____

Which ones would you be willing to change? _____

_____

Which ones would you like to strengthen? _____

_____

Fear of the unknown

Roger nurtures an overriding desire for security and order and an intolerance for chaos. He's deeply afraid of failure and the risks involved in an ambiguous and unknown future. He refuses to programme his life around planning assumptions, because he sees no guarantee that those assumptions will turn out the way he wants them to. He's so obsessed with surviving in the present that he can't bring himself to prepare for the future. He avoids the chance of making a mistake by closely adhering to his time-tested operating routines.

What do you fear most about the future? _____

_____

How does this fear keep you from being successful? ———

_____

Lack of perseverance
Successful planners become so firmly committed to their plans for the future that they're able to resist any and all distractions that threaten the accomplishment of their intended goals. But not Becky. She can't stick to a predetermined course of action, no matter how well it's spelled out. She gives up easily when faced with even the slightest obstacle.

The difference between Becky and people who plan successfully is as explicable as the difference in people's ability to solve intellectual problems or perform acts of skill.

Becky recognises her shortcomings, including her lack of perseverance in the face of difficulty. But she'll never get started until she understands and applies the basic elements of the planning process and sticks to a simple planning strategy.

Have you ever given in when the going got tough, only to find out later that things weren't as bad as you thought they were?

_____

_____

_____

_____

Key ingredients for successful planning

There is, and always will be, a significant difference between people who find success in planning and those who rely on the fickle finger of fate to get ahead. The biggest difference can be found in the following personality traits. Successful planners reflect these traits. Non-planners generally don't have them.

Curiosity
Good planners take time to work out why things are as they seem to be. They seek answers to questions about the future and try to gauge their chances of success against the unknown. Are you curious? Yes ☐ Not very ☐

Creativity
Good planners look for new ideas, new strategies or new ways of applying old ideas to current issues. Are you creative? Yes ☐ Not very ☐

Competitiveness
Good planners enjoy intellectual competition and are skilled at verbal give-and-take. They look for strengths and weaknesses in other people's ideas and test contradictory positions against their own. Do you like to compete?
Yes ☐ Not very much ☐

Practicality
Good planners are realistic, enthusiastic and very pragmatic about their chances of success. They know what can be done, how fast it can be completed, and what they have to do to finish it. Are you practical? Yes ☐ Not very ☐

Confidence
Good planners can cope with criticism and rejection from any quarter. Logic and reason help them to persevere, no matter what the odds. Do you have confidence in yourself?
Yes ☐ Not very much ☐

Wisdom
Good planners keep up with developments in all fields of knowledge, especially those that affect their goals and objectives. Do you try to learn something new every day?
Yes ☐ Not always ☐

Persistence
Good planners are so committed to their well-tuned plans that they're able to overcome just about any obstacle or threat

that stands in their way. Do you keep going when the going gets tough? Yes ☐ Not always ☐

If you think you lack any of these successful-planner traits, then make up your mind right now to add them to your repertoire. They'll give you the power you need to conquer what you've long thought are virtually impossible obstacles.

Write out your resolution in the space below.

I intend to increase my ————————————————————

—————————————————————————————————

And while you're at it, make a concerted effort to understand the relationship between chance, luck and planning.

Chance, luck and planning

You learned earlier that chance is made up of an infinite number of unforeseeable happenings – both great and small – that are constantly taking place in the world around you. Chance events happen unexpectedly, without apparent human intervention or observable cause. These events cannot be planned, predicted or prearranged.

With more and more people living in less and less space, and moving about more rapidly than ever, you are bound to experience more unpredictable encounters, more strange coincidences and more fortuitous events. But the more unexpected chances you run into, the more opportunities you'll have to be lucky.

You cannot know the cause of everything that happens around you, nor can you accurately predict every event that might affect your future. But you can make some educated guesses. And once you've made those guesses, you can make plans to encounter chance events whenever they cross your path.

Success doesn't happen by chance alone. It comes from hard work and planning. If successful people seem lucky, it's because they plan ahead to take advantage of every opportunity that comes their way.

By now you have a good understanding of the planning process and of all the advantages and disadvantages that go with it. And you understand why some people choose not to plan. You should also have a pretty good idea of the promise that planning holds for *your* future. What you need now are some tips on how to put it all together. That's coming up next.

CHAPTER 3
How to Plan

You've been introduced to some of the fundamentals of planning, and a number of reasons why some short-sighted people choose not to plan. Now you're probably all set to do some planning of your own. But before you get involved with a major project, you should run through a few preliminary concepts to give yourself a better base from which to start. This chapter contains some things you ought to know about risk, luck, contingencies, assumptions, performance measures and endings.

The element of risk

Risk is the measured possibility of experiencing a loss, an injury or some other unfavourable outcome. Insurance companies use risk factors to determine how much they're going to charge for their policies.

You face calculated risks every day of your life in everything you do, including the risk of being in a road accident, catching a cold or losing money on the stock market. They're called calculated risks because you take the risk knowingly. You have calculated the advantages versus disadvantages.

In planning for the future, you have to know something about the risks you face and the chances you have of being successful. You especially need to know how much risk you can afford and still be comfortable with what you're doing.

Let's assume that you have been assigned a project that consists of five separate events, each of which has an 80 per cent chance of success. That means that for any single event, your risk of failure is only two in ten.

That sounds pretty good, doesn't it? But it may surprise you to know that your chance of success for all five events taken together is not 80 per cent, but only 33 per cent, or *one in three*.

Calculating your chance of success for a planned project that is made up of several events is fairly simple. You multiply the odds of being successful in the first event by the odds of the second event by the odds of the third event, on down the line. In this case, multiplying 80 per cent (0.80) by itself five times turns out to be 33 per cent (0.33). To increase the probability of your five-event project to 80 per cent, you'd have to increase the probability of success for each event to almost 96 per cent.

Obviously, a simple plan, where only a few things can go wrong, will reduce your risks and give you a much better chance of being successful than one with several independent events. But no matter what the odds are, you'll still be a lot better off if you planned than if you cast your lot to the winds and hoped for the best.

Luck and planning

You can improve your luck, reduce your risks and enhance your prospects of being successful by understanding the interplay between external chance and inward response.

A chance event, like meeting a helpful stranger or discovering a new piece of information, can shape your luck and determine your success, but it will not affect you unless you respond to it. Your response will be determined in large part by your needs, attitudes and patterns of behaviour that have evolved throughout your lifetime.

How do you react to people you've never met before that sit next to you on the bus? Is it possible that you and they might share interlocking needs that could be satisfied to your mutual satisfaction? You'll never know if you hide your face in the newspaper and never attempt any contact.

But what happens if you do introduce yourself and find that there is a possibility for future involvement? The more you know about what you really want and the better prepared you are, the better you'll be at applying yourself when a favourable chance appears. You'll also have more chances because you'll improve your ability to identify them. And the more chances you have, the more luck you'll have.

> The key to improving your luck lies in planning – the process of identifying the strengths, interests and personal qualities you would like to develop and applying those characteristics whenever you get an opportunity.

Planning will help you to maintain a high level of readiness. You'll recognise good fortune when it appears, you'll take advantage of the opportunity it presents, and experience a tremendous surge of fulfilment that will stay with you for a long time to come.

Just say 'Hullo' the next time you meet someone new in a non-threatening situation – on the bus, on a train, at a party – and see what happens.

Planning for contingencies

A contingency is something that might happen, but then again, it might not. If it does occur, it will generally be when you least expect it. A flat tyre, an unexpected guest, a sudden drop in the stock market, or a broken water heater are all examples of contingencies.

Contingencies can completely immobilise you if you're tied to complicated and unresponsive plans. Inflexible schedules don't allow for spontaneous actions when an unexpected monkey wrench gets thrown in the works.

Contingency plans don't have to be elaborate. Having a spare tyre in your car qualifies. So does a well-balanced investment plan. Just follow the Boy Scout motto and 'Be Prepared'.

Why not take a minute now and think about some of the contingency plans you already have in place. Make a list of them in the box provided.

My current contingency plans

1. _____

2. _____

3. _____

4. _____

One good thing about having a contingency plan is that its very existence, and the approach it implies, helps to guarantee that you'll never need it. Your awareness of potential problems will keep you in a state of readiness that can usually prevent a contingency from ever happening in the first place.

Contingencies can sometimes enhance a planned course of action, especially when they force you to find creative solutions to the problems they present. The demands these spontaneous outbursts make of you can enrich your understanding of the planning process and increase your chances for a successful outcome.

Planning assumptions

A planning assumption is something that you think is true or that you just take for granted. It's an intuitive feeling you have about what you think is going to happen in the next few weeks, months or years.

Planning assumptions are based on investigative findings that relate to you and the world you live in. These assumptions can involve anything you think will have an impact on your life, including economic conditions (recessions, growth), anticipated business developments (mergers, expansions), or changes in your social life (marriage, divorce). They are the foundation upon which you develop the goals and objectives of your plan.

Take a minute now and write down six assumptions that you think could have a definite impact on your plans for the future.

Six important planning assumptions

1. _____

2. _____

3. _____

4. _____

5. _____

6. _____

Performance measures

You've probably asked yourself from time to time whether or not you're heading in the right direction. Or you've wondered, after reaching a goal, if you've been successful or not.

Sometimes it's easy to see what you've done. You've lost 15 pounds or you haven't. You've saved £1000 or you haven't. You received your promotion or you didn't.

These objectives are fairly easy to measure. But you won't know if your plans are falling into place or not if you don't already have some way to measure your performance. So _before_ you start to implement your plan, be sure you know what you're going to measure and how you're going to do it.

Here are some measures you can use to assess your performance. They'll help you to work out how well you're doing while you're carrying out your plan of action.

1. _Your previous history of success and failure_
    Are you doing better or worse (happier, sadder, richer, poorer) than you've done in the past?

2. _Levels of achievement you think are possible_
    How much, how many, how far, how long?

3. *Expectations of people who are evaluating you, and your feelings about those evaluations*
   What are you expected to do and for whom?

4. *Actual progress, as measured by facts and figures*
   How many pounds, marks, points?

5. *The cost in time and other resources needed to reach your goals and objectives*
   Are the benefits more or less than the costs?

Example
Here's an example. Let's say your goal is to increase your sales from £80,000 to £125,000 a year. Which of these measures of success would you use?

- Number of pounds   _____
- Rapport with customers   _____
- Respect of your colleagues   _____
- Admiration from your family   _____
- Increased self-worth   _____
- (Others) _____

What about sacrifices? Tick those you wouldn't want to take on, no matter what the rewards might be.

- More studying or training   _____
- Reduced leisure time   _____
- Longer working hours   _____
- More time away from home and family   _____
- Head on competition with a friend   _____
- (Others)_____

The best indicator of success is your enhanced self-image, the set of values you hold for yourself. You can measure your present self-image by asking some basic questions like these:

1. Are you proud of your accomplishments?
   Yes _____ Room for improvement _____

2. Have you gained self-esteem by sticking to your plan and reaching your goals and objectives?
   Yes _____ Room for improvement _____

3. What is your status among the groups and individuals that are important to you?
   High _____ Room for improvement _____

Endings

One of the most important things you can do while mapping out your future is to toss out the concept of a single, perfect ending to a well-orchestrated set of plans. You may reach your original goal, but if you have steered your thoughts and actions down one narrow, singleminded channel, you'll miss out on one of the greatest rewards of planning.

Life is a complex array of never-ending pathways that lead off in all directions. The routes you choose will be determined by your goals and objectives and the success you have in carrying out your plans.

You may start out on one path and end up on an entirely different one. Or you might see your original goal in a totally different light than when you first set out to reach it. Instead of an ending, your original goal may appear as the beginning of a new quest for yet another goal that will seem even more important than the last.

For example, you might set out to become an office manager. But as that goal comes closer to reality, you might begin to think of it only as a milestone towards another goal such as becoming a director, starting your own company, or going back to college.

Each new goal will bring with it the challenge and excitement of a chase. There will be new stars to shoot for and new dreams of things to come. That's what keeps planning interesting and keeps you growing.

CHAPTER 4

Strategies for Success

Now let's get down to specifics. The strategies on the following pages will help to prepare you for planning, show you the difference between good and bad planning, and give you the tools you need to reach your goals and objectives. But first assess your planning skills.

Quiz yourself

Answer each of the following questions about yourself. They will help you to develop a clear picture of where you are now and what you want to do in the future.

- What are the most significant events that have happened to you in the past three to five years? Why do you think they're important? _____

  _____

- What is your record of successes and failures? _____

  _____

- What's your position in the world today? _____

  _____

- How well are you performing? _____

  _____

- What results can you expect from your present activities? _____

- What have you sown? What will you reap? _____

- What do you want to be when you grow up? _____

- How high do you want to go up the ladder of success?

- What are your three most important goals in life? ____

- What is your philosophy of life? _____

- How are you going to get where you want to go? ____

- What tools and resources will you need to get there?

- What tools and resources should you keep? _____

- What tools and resources should you throw away? ____

- How will you know when you've completed the stages you've identified? _____

Your answers will not only give you a better understanding of your capabilities and limitations, they'll also give you a realistic idea of some of the opportunities that are open to you.

You can broaden your perspective, enhance your planning activities and improve your chances of success even more by getting additional information from friends, relatives, loved ones, and business associates.

Determine your strengths

This exercise will help you to start developing your plans for the future.

On the next page, write down all the *things you're good at*; deeds you've done that have earned you praise from other people or have given you a lot of satisfaction.

List things like making money, speaking in public, playing a musical instrument, taking part in sporting events, building objects with your hands, or selling products or ideas to other people. Include intangible strengths like values, self-esteem, work attitudes, willingness to accept risk and other attributes that set you apart from the crowd.

Be objective. Don't put down qualities you just wish you had, and don't ignore characteristics you think are not important.

Then write down the *things you enjoy doing* whether you're good at them or not.

List things like hiking, camping, travelling, playing tennis, managing money, closing a sale, chairing a meeting, completing a report or meeting new people.

The areas of strength that will have the greatest impact on your future success are those related to your health, intelligence, experience, motivation, personal appearance, talents and skills.

If you can go through these two lists and concentrate on doing things you're good at *and* enjoy, your chances of success will increase tremendously.

Things I'm good at doing

1. _____

2. _____

3. _____

4. _____

5. _____

6. _____

7. _____

8. _____

Things I enjoy doing

1. _____

2. _____

3. _____

4. _____

5. _____

6. _____

7. _____

8. _____

Determine your weaknesses

This exercise is just as important as the last one, so give it lots of serious thought.

On the next page, write down things *you're not very good at* or that you just can't seem to develop a knack for doing.

Personal habits like getting to work on time, sticking with a task until it's done, paying attention in staff meetings, or communicating with colleagues can all affect your planning success if you're not very good at them, so be sure to include them as weaknesses. But don't put down things like computer programming or sales management if you've never done them before.

Then write down *things you don't enjoy doing*, like getting up early, writing up sales reports, staying in the office or talking on the telephone. Put down anything you'd avoid doing if you could.

Include physical as well as mental avoidances that keep you from moving ahead. Add things like exercising and cutting down on smoking, over-eating or drinking too much. And be honest with yourself. It's better to identify problem areas before you get started than to discover them after you're hopelessly bogged down in an impossible journey.

Weaknesses that involve interactions with family, friends and social contacts are as important as those involving business associates. They can all affect your ability to succeed, so include them wherever you can.

You've probably already realised that if you can avoid doing things you don't like to do or are not very good at, you'll have a much better chance of being successful.

Things I'm not very good at doing

1. _____

2. _____

3. _____

4. _____

5. _____

6. _____

7. _____

8. _____

Things I don't enjoy doing

1. _____

2. _____

3. _____

4. _____

5. _____

6. _____

7. _____

8. _____

Itemise opportunities

The mental aerobics continue.

In the space below, write down every idea, situation or circumstance you can think of that will enhance your chances of success. If the competition is weak and you are strong, put that down as an opportunity. If you're doing something you enjoy and are good at, put that down on the same list. Include intangible opportunities, such as the area in which you live, the reputation you have in your commmunity or your relationships with other people.

Opportunities I have

1. _____

2. _____

3. _____

4. _____

5. _____

6. _____

7. _____

8. _____

Itemise threats

On the next page, write down anything you can think of that might frustrate your efforts, slow down your progress or sidetrack your drive for success. Include your competitors if they're stronger than you. Add your lack of expertise if you're just starting out. If you're in a highly competitive business and have only a small clientele, put that down.

Threats I face

1. _____
2. _____
3. _____
4. _____
5. _____
6. _____
7. _____
8. _____

Compare your lists

Now you've got four lists of what you see as strengths, weaknesses, opportunities and threats. The next step is to combine the items on those lists in a way that will help you to plan your future and reach your dreams of success.

Use the table below as a guide.

	Opportunities	Threats
Strengths	A	B
Weaknesses	C	D

First, look at your strengths – the things you like to do and are good at – and your opportunities. Determine which opportunities exist because of your strengths and which strengths exist only because of the opportunities you have available. Those are the combinations you'll find in Box **A**. Take these combinations and work with them, because they have the greatest potential for your growth.

An opportunity may exist because you lack competition, have a lot of customers and carry a good product line.

Combine that opportunity with your willingness to work hard and your ability to sell things to other people, and you'll increase your chances of being a successful salesperson. Opportunities and strengths will always work to your advantage if you recognise their relationship and can capitalise on it.

Now combine your weaknesses – the things you don't like to do, or tend to screw up from time to time – with your list of threats. They come together in Box **D** of the chart. Some threats exist only because of your weaknesses, and some weaknesses exist only because of threats you've identified. Flag those combinations, because they can cause some of your biggest problems.

Imagine, as an example, the threat of not being able to move ahead in your job. Combine that threat with the possible weakness of not having a degree. Add the problems you have in taking examinations and your inability to concentrate on difficult tasks. It shouldn't be hard to see that if you were saddled with a combination like that, you wouldn't generate much success. You'd be better off looking for another job or trying to develop some new skills.

Your comparison table
Now fill in Box **A** and Box **D** of the table overleaf, using your own strengths and opportunities and your own weaknesses and threats.

Don't try to match your list of strengths against your list of threats in Box **B**. And *don't* try to take advantage of an opportunity by doing things you aren't good at or don't like to do, as in Box **C**. Concentrate instead on combining your strengths with obvious opportunities, while avoiding combinations of weaknesses and threats. If you're successful in making these combinations, you'll spend 80 to 90 per cent of your time doing what you want to do in situations that are going to *help* you, and only 10 to 20 per cent of your time doing things you don't enjoy doing or aren't very good at. As you can see, the odds will be in your favour.

	Opportunities	Threats
Strengths	A _____ _____ _____ _____ _____ _____ _____ _____ _____	B
Weaknesses	C	D _____ _____ _____ _____ _____ _____ _____ _____ _____

Go over your lists of weaknesses and threats from time to time and see where you can avoid or eliminate them altogether, especially where they work against you and keep you from being successful.

Know what you want to do

If you don't know where you're going, you'll probably end up somewhere else.

Do a little brainstorming and write down every success-generating strength and opportunity idea you can think of, no matter how far-fetched it may seem when it first comes to mind. Give each of your ideas serious consideration because sudden and spontaneous insight and seat-of-the-pants impressions can be very productive. Follow your intuition, but don't let it overrule objective decision-making. If your newly hatched ideas fail to hold water, discard them and open your mind again to other thoughts.

Strength – Opportunity ideas

1. _____
2. _____
3. _____
4. _____
5. _____
6. _____

Now rewrite general ideas as specific tasks that can be done right away. Tear into them without hesitation. They'll keep you on your toes, stop you from procrastinating and give you a good start on your trek to a rewarding future.

1. _____
2. _____
3. _____
4. _____
5. _____
6. _____

Develop goals and objectives

Goals and objectives are the stepping stones to success and the footings upon which all planning is based. Without them, your hopes for a happy and prosperous future stand little chance of being fulfilled.

Goals are broad, long-term, idealistic statements of hoped-for accomplishments. Objectives are clear, concise statements of activities you want to complete in specific time periods. Your goal may be a wistful desire to lose an unspecified amount of weight. Your objective would be to start today to lose seven pounds within a three-week period. Objectives are almost always measured by how much, how far, how big or how many. That makes it easier to tell whether you've reached them or not.

Goals and objectives should be realistic, attainable, challenging and measurable. They should represent things you really want and are willing to work for. They can either be positive or negative, and they can either drive you towards something or away from it. If your goal is to lose weight, you may want to look slimmer (positive goal) or avoid looking fat (negative goal).

Five major life goals

Take a minute now and, in the box opposite, write down five major goals you would like to accomplish in the near to distant future. For each goal, write down as many specific objectives as you think would be appropriate. Don't worry about making them 'just right'. You'll learn how to do that as you go through the rest of this chapter. Just get them down for now and then come back to them as you get a better understanding of the process.

Life is dynamic, fluctuating and always changing, so goals and objectives have to be flexible or they won't be of much use. If they're not renewed from time to time, they'll soon be out of date and lose their importance. If a goal is unreachable, back off and establish a more realistic outcome. If a goal looks too easy, raise your sights and try for something bigger.

Landmarks are passed from time to time as you progress towards your overall objectives. If your landmarks are close together, you'll arrive at them sooner and satisfy your short-term goals more quickly. That will boost your morale, give you a greater sense of accomplishment, and generate the enthusiasm you'll need to reach your overall goal.

My five major goals in life

1. _____

   Objectives: _____

   _____

2. _____

   Objectives: _____

   _____

3. _____

   Objectives: _____

   _____

4. _____

   Objectives: _____

   _____

5. _____

   Objectives: _____

   _____

Establish your criteria

It's not easy to measure how successful you are in meeting your goals and objectives unless you have some standards upon which to base your decisions.

Goals and objectives should be as specific as possible without being too restrictive. If you're going on a diet, say how many pounds you want to lose, don't just say you want to lose weight. If you're going to ask for a pay increase, work out how much you need and negotiate for that amount. If you're trying to finish a work-related project, know how much you have to complete at each landmark. Spell out your goals so you know exactly what you're shooting for.

Avoid exaggerations, misconceptions, idealistic terms, oversimplifications, opinions that are subject to change, understated or overstated words and terms that have a wide range of meaning. Use precise terms so you never have any doubts about what you're doing. But stay flexible so you can change your goals whenever it becomes necessary. You'll need to fine-tune your objectives from time to time to keep them up to date.

Take one of the five goals you listed earlier, and write it down more specifically in the space below. Add specific objectives and landmarks.

Goal _____

Objective 1 _____

Landmarks _____

Objective 2 _____

Landmarks _____

Objective 3 _____

Landmarks _____

Think of the methods you're going to use and the resources you'll consume in reaching your goal. If you're dieting, list the foods you will avoid or the supplements you will take. If you're looking for a job advancement, list the courses you will take or the books you'll read. Identify every reasonable course of action that's available to you (for example, diets and exercise, or college courses and personal counselling). Weigh the advantages and disadvantages of each (the costs and benefits), then decide which ones hold the most promise.

METHODS:	Advantages	Disadvantages
1. _____	_____	_____
2. _____	_____	_____
3. _____	_____	_____

RESOURCES:	Advantages	Disadvantages
1. _____	_____	_____
2. _____	_____	_____
3. _____	_____	_____

Now translate your chosen course of action into a concise statement of what you're going to do.

What I'm going to do: _____

How I'm going to do it: best method _____

best resource(s) _____

When I'm going to do it: _____

Where I'm going to do it: _____

Why I'm going to do it: _____

Write down what you're going to do on a piece of paper. Keep it in front of you so you're always aware of what you're trying to do. Attach a copy to your bathroom mirror. Paste one on your refrigerator door. Stick a copy to the dashboard of your car. Hang one over your desk.

Clarify your plan

Identify the major steps you have to take to reach your goals by listing sharply defined objectives. If your plan is laid out clearly in front of you, you'll know where you've been, where you are now, and where you're headed in the future.

Streamline your plan so it's easy to follow. Avoid overlap, conflict and duplication. Take reasonable short cuts when you see them, and pass over any unnecessary tasks that get in your way. Be sure to have a contingency plan ready in case something goes wrong.

Determine how you will decide when you've reached an objective and how well you did in getting there. Consider things like weight lost, knowledge gained, promotions received or salary increases picked up. Set your expectations early, but be ready to revise them if your situation changes.

Manage your time

Time gives substance to your plans. It tells you when some things ought to be done, and it reminds you when it's too late to do others. If you don't have a personal organiser to guide your efforts, your plans will seem like meaningless meanderings.

Manage time like money. Keep track of what you use, and balance your diary the way you balance your bank account. Know how much you can do in a specified time. Set aside prime time for the really important tasks. Maintain a tight schedule to keep you from dawdling and procrastinating. Consolidate your efforts in the time you have, then watch your productivity go up.

Your deadlines should be precise but flexible. Over-ambitious deadlines can inspire you to greater efforts or they can cause you to take dangerous side trips. Easy deadlines lead to procrastination. Indefinite deadlines are too easily ignored.

Schedule activities and events over different periods so everything doesn't happen at once. Identify specific dates (days, weeks, months or years) on which designated targets will be reached and specific objectives will be attained. Keep big and little achievements happening on a regular basis. They'll add variety to your programme and give you a feeling of continuous accomplishment.

The more short-term success you can generate, the more control you'll have over the whole planning process. So develop lots of day-to-day objectives where you have a good chance of being successful. Build on these successful outcomes by incorporating your most productive methods into your overall programme for reaching long-range goals.

Schedule

Look back at the objectives and landmarks you listed in the exercise on page 51. In the space below, construct a schedule for them, adding as many short-term objectives as you can.

**Achieve by
(date)**

Goal _____ _____

Objective _____ _____

Landmarks _____ _____

_____ _____

_____ _____

Objective _____ _____

Landmarks _____ _____

_____ _____

_____ _____

Objective _____ _____

Landmarks _____ _____

_____ _____

_____ _____

Objective _____ _____

Landmarks _____ _____

_____ _____

_____ _____

Objective _____ _____

Landmarks _____ _____

_____ _____

_____ _____

CHAPTER 5
Hints and Tips

This chapter offers some useful tips, from playing the odds to priming the pump. When you've worked through it, you'll be physically and emotionally ready to set your plan in motion. You'll know what makes a good plan and a good planner. You'll be able to recognise some of the probable causes of failure and know how to avoid them.

Remember, plan for the problems you hope will never come. And whenever opportunity knocks, be sure you're there to answer the door.

Play the odds

Planning and poker have a lot in common. They both call for decisions that are based on incomplete and sometimes inaccurate information, and they're both affected by chance. You'll see a lot more success in your planning efforts if you know what your odds are and what cards you hold before you enter the game. You should also be able to use the principles of probability to your advantage.

What are your odds of winning a lottery? How many other people are aiming for the same promotion as you? How many customers are in your territory and what are the odds of your landing a sale rather than three other suppliers?

Use analytical methods to examine your imaginative hunches. If you're hoping to increase your sales by 20 per cent, check available census data and make sure the customers are really out there. Build your tolerance for risk by concentrating on events where the odds are in your favour.

Avoid activities where success seems impossible. Change your strategy whenever you think it will improve your odds.

Assign priorities

An important task is one that yields a high return for the time invested and clearly contributes to the achievement of your long-term goals and objectives.

An urgent task is simply one that calls for immediate action. It could be a complete waste of time.

Go through your list of things to do and ask yourself if each task is moving you closer to a lifetime goal or if it's sending you off in the wrong direction. Put an asterisk(*) by the tasks that are directly related to your goals and then arrange them in order of priority.

Put tasks that are important *and* urgent at the top of your list. Give the next highest priority to important, non-urgent tasks. Start each day by doing those things that give you the most pleasure and provide the biggest pay-off.

Sometimes it makes sense to work on a task that's less urgent or important than another. It could be something as simple as taking a walk to reduce job stress. If it doesn't take much time, and if the benefits are substantial, it could serve as a warm-up exercise for more important tasks.

Don't stop to establish priorities every time you're ready to begin a new task. Your day will be much more productive if you assign your priorities the night before you go to work or first thing in the morning when you arrive at your desk. You'll be in better control of your time and you'll know that important things are being tended to.

Re-examine your priorities from time to time and feel free to change them if you have a good reason for doing so. Don't be afraid to say 'no' to unimportant tasks that can disrupt your overall strategy. Keep your goals first and foremost in your mind so you don't get caught in the trap of overestimating the importance of what you're doing.

Make sure your priorities are realistic and well-suited to your goal. When you're standing knee-deep in alligators, it's hard to remember that you were supposed to clean the swamp.

You'll find an excellent exercise in Chapter 6. It will help you set to priorities for any project you're working on.

Dynamic imaging

You can reach any goal faster and better if you can create in your mind's eye a clear and vivid image of yourself getting it done. The key lies in the intensity of your vision and the depth of your concentration.

Many professional golfers, before they swing, will create a visual image of their ball hitting the green and dropping into the cup. Downhill ski racers, before they start, will try to visualise themselves making every gate and crossing the finish line in record time.

The technique is called *dynamic imaging*. It can work as well for you as for anyone. You just have to avoid overblown standards and unreasonable expectations, and think only about realistic goals and objectives you know you can accomplish.

Picture yourself as an attractively thin person if you're trying to lose weight. Picture yourself in graduation garb if you're a struggling undergraduate. See yourself as a happy spouse, a successful business person, or as anything else you'd like to be.

Your ability to recall visual stimuli is limited only by your imagination. You can enhance your vision by approaching your goals and objectives with all your senses. Taste them, smell them, see them, hear them and touch them if you can. Anything is worth doing if it gets you closer to your desired outcomes.

Make a commitment

Formalise your responsibilities in a commitment. Tell yourself – and others – that you're going to dedicate every resource to the attainment of your goal. Put it in writing and then share it with your spouse, parents, children, siblings, colleagues, a favourite mentor or others whom you trust and respect. They'll not only share your enthusiasm, they'll help to determine your strengths and weaknesses, assess your progress and evaluate your results.

Believe in what you're doing and in the goals you have chosen to pursue. Establish a climate that's conducive to change. Innovate wherever you can. Concentrate on long-term goals, but take pleasure in short-term accomplishments. Carry out your plan with vim, vigour and vitality. Convince yourself that the journey you're about to embark on is one you really want to tackle and that you're fully capable of seeing it through.

A friend of mine once carved his long-term goal on a silver coin and kept it with him always. He looked at it every day and shared its message with people who believed in him. He was so focused on his goal that he reached it several years before he or anyone else expected him to. You can do the same.

Start when ready

Don't get so wrapped up in the process of planning that you fail to recognise when it's time to start moving. I have neighbours who once spent so much time planning a trip to Disney World that they literally did not get their car out of the garage before their holiday time was up.

Make sure your first task is an easy one, especially if it's going to take a tremendous amount of energy for you to get out of the starting blocks. That first task should break the bonds of inertia, get you off dead centre, and lead you right into the thick of the hunt.

Work at it

The only place where success comes before work is in the dictionary.

Recognise peak performance periods and use them for working on really difficult tasks. Save routine work for less productive times. Prune back any unnecessary tasks that slow you down and distract you from your overall goal. Maintain a consistent level of effort and concentrate on what you're doing.

Success is habit forming. If you work hard at being good in one area of your life, your success will carry over into every other area you're involved in. You'll not only make tremendous progress, you'll be in a better position to handle any unexpected problems that might arise.

Take time, whenever you reach a landmark, to survey where you are, what you've done to get there, and what you have to do to keep moving ahead. Reflect on your accomplishments and see how well you have done. Incorporate today's insights into tomorrow's strategies.

Document any unexpected events that spring up along the way. Pinpoint what strategies work best and refer to them whenever your progress is slowed or blocked. Gather a storehouse of information about your progress and use it where it will do the most good.

If you're like most people, you do 80 per cent of your most productive work in 20 per cent of the time you have available. That leaves plenty of time for adjustments and improvements. Fill in that extra time with special tasks. Build a sense of improvement into your expectations and work hard at doing better day by day.

Stay flexible

Everything around you is changing, so even a well-drawn plan may be out of date by the time you put it to use. In fact, many skilled planners maintain that the only plan that's 100 per cent up to date is one that's just been changed.

Diversity is the best protection against catastrophe. That's another way of telling you not to put all your eggs in one basket. Have some alternative strategies ready in case your initial plan doesn't work out. Replace strategies that fail to live up to your expectations.

Keep analysing the interaction between your strengths, weaknesses, opportunities and threats, even after you've reached some preliminary goals and objectives. Stay flexible and keep thinking about the challenges that lie ahead. Postpone judgement of what is and what is not important until you reach the point where you can deal with new ideas without prejudice. You'll find it easier to think up alternative courses of action if it looks as though changes in strategy might be helpful.

Don't take spectacular leaps unless you're a trapeze artist. Recognise and use the power of patience. You can see it all around you in the flowering of a rose, in the growing of a tree. They don't happen in an instant, but in bits and pieces over time. Learn from Mother Nature. She's been working at it for a long time.

Know your world

Look around you for critical ingredients of success and key factors of growth. Recognise leaders and role models who have an impact on your life. Describe the effect they have on the way you feel about yourself and the way you approach your goals.

Compare your attitude and skills with those of your colleagues, competitors and others to see if you have what it takes to hold your own against the tide. See if you're operating at their level, doing better than they are, or trailing far behind. Find out if other, more successful people are doing things that you could do just as well. See if you can incorporate their techniques and strategies into your own plans for success.

Know how you relate to the individuals you work with or those who are involved in your personal life. Are you the big wheel or just part of the crowd? Are there bigger or smaller fish in your pond? Size up your relationship with everyone who is going to have a significant impact on your designs for the future and incorporate your findings into the strategies you choose to follow.

CHAPTER 6

Your Plan of Action

You've designed your hoped-for future and, by spelling out your goals and objectives, you've taken the first few steps towards getting there. Now you're ready for action. All you have to do is carry out your plan.

Decide what parts of your plan are most important and set out to do those first. Organise your tasks around a realistic timetable so you can get a better idea of what you have to do and when you have to do it. Work out how to measure your performance so you'll be able to see how well you've done. And be sure you know what the odds are for coming out ahead of the pack.

Eight strategies

Here are eight initial planning strategies that will help you to get started towards a successful future.

1. Develop the planning habit
Plan everything you do until the process becomes automatic. Start with simple day-to-day errands, then work your way up to lifetime goals and objectives. Know which tasks have the highest priority and do those first. Leave no more to chance than is absolutely necessary.

2. Find a way
Your physical surroundings and the people around you should contribute to your planning efforts, not frustrate them. So find a place where you'll be encouraged to plan.

Experiment with different settings. Work alone or with someone. Ask for suggestions or keep to yourself. See what works best for you and use it wherever you can.

3. Get help
Know what you have to do to complete your tasks and what kind of help you're going to need from others. Delegate complete authority and responsibility to people who know what you're doing and who are willing to help. Give them crystal-clear instructions, then back off and let them do the best they can.

4. Be accurate
Base your plans on concrete facts and real situations. Know the difference between the way things are and the way you want them to be. Get the best information available, then draw up realistic estimates of your chances for success.

5. Be perceptive
Be on the alert for new opportunities and take advantage of them whenever you can. Anticipate obstacles and devise effective means of getting rid of them. Develop alternative plans to deal with contingencies. Know where you are every step of the way.

6. Keep it simple
Your plan should be simple, well organised and clearly understood. Tasks and activities should be well defined, timetables should be realistic and resources should be attainable.

7. Get better
Don't leave your planning to chance. If you don't have the skill, discipline or expertise to carry out your plans, then take time to acquire them. Strive for greater competence through daily practice and additional study.

8. Be flexible

Be responsive to every possibility. Modify, change or revise your plans if they prove to be unworkable or obsolete. Avoid the functionally and psychologically destructive stress of inflexibility.

Summary: the eight basic steps

Earlier, you were introduced to the eight basic steps of the planning process. Here they are again in abbreviated form. They provide an excellent framework upon which you can develop everything you need for a plan of action.

1. Assessment

Determine where you are now and where you want to be in the future. Clarify your need to be successful in whatever endeavours you choose to pursue.

2. Commitment

Cross your heart and hope to die that you'll start work *now* on a plan for the future.

3. Investigation

Take a look at yourself from every angle and write down what you find. Develop a profile of who you are and what you want to be.

4. Decision

Make up your mind about what you want to do and when you want to do it.

5. Organisation

Develop some specific goals and objectives and set a timetable for carrying them out.

6. Preparation

Gather together all the resources you will need to carry out your plan of action.

7. Implementation

Launch a leading task that will put your plan in motion and follow up on everything you do.

8. Achievement

Grab the prize.

Establishing priorities

The easiest way to satisfy your goals and objectives is by doing things that are really important and have the highest priority. The hard part is deciding how to prioritise your tasks. Here's an easy way to do it.

Let's assume that you have already identified ten major task areas:

- Catch up on correspondence
- Recapture lost sales revenue
- Take the new sales representative to lunch
- Evaluate clerical staff performance
- Prepare new product information
- Reconcile expense reports
- Attend a meeting of the board of directors
- Meet the shareholders' committee
- Plan the company open day
- Stocktake.

You'd like to give all of them your undivided attention, but you just don't have the time. So you have to concentrate on some at the expense of others. You know four of the tasks are not only important, but urgent as well, so you assign them top priority right away.

High priority items

- Recapture lost sales revenue
- Prepare new product information
- Attend a meeting of the board of directors
- Meet the shareholders' committee.

That leaves six tasks you're not sure about.

Questionable tasks

- Catch up on correspondence
- Take the new sales representative to lunch
- Evaluate clerical staff performance
- Reconcile expense reports
- Plan the company open day
- Stocktake.

You need to compare each of these six with all the others. In each case, you decide – if the choice had to be one or the other – which one you would opt to work on in the limited amount of time you have. First, compare 'Catch up on correspondence' with each of the five other tasks.

You can make your comparison on any basis you choose: more versus less enjoyable, difficult or rewarding – or because the boss expects it to be done. You should set your criteria according to how critical the task is in helping you to reach your intended goal. In this case it may be a hoped-for promotion. Just don't change your criteria in the middle of your ranking.

Here's the first set of comparisons:

— Correspondence or sales rep? *Sales rep.*

— Correspondence or clerical staff? *Clerical staff.*

— Correspondence or expense reports? *Expense reports.*

— Correspondence or open day? *Correspondence.*

— Correspondence or stock? *Stock.*

Next, compare 'Take the new sales representative to lunch' with the four remaining tasks:

— Sales rep or clerical staff? *Clerical staff.*

— Sales rep or expense reports? *Expense reports.*

— Sales rep or open day? *Sales rep.*

— Sales rep or stock? *Sales rep.*

Then compare 'Evaluate clerical staff performance' with the three remaining tasks:

— Clerical staff or expense reports? *Clerical staff.*

— Clerical staff or open day? *Clerical staff.*

— Clerical staff or stock? *Clerical staff.*

Compare 'Reconcile expense reports' with the two remaining tasks:

— Expense reports or open day? *Expense reports.*

— Expense reports or stock? *Expense reports.*

Finally, compare the last two items:

— Open day or stock? *Open day.*

Now add the number of times each task was chosen, and rank the tasks from highest to lowest. In this example, evaluating clerical staff was chosen 5 times, reconciling expense reports was chosen 4 times, and having lunch with the new sales representative 3 times. Catching up on correspondence, planning the company open day and taking stock of supplies all tied at 1.

If two are tied, look at their head-to-head comparison and give the one that was selected over the other the highest priority. When three are tied, as in this case, try to force one out or consider them all as deserving equal treatment.

Here is the new, prioritised list.

1. Recapture lost sales revenue

2. Prepare new product information

3. Attend a meeting of the board of directors

4. Meet the shareholders' committee

5. Evaluate clerical staff performance

6. Reconcile expense reports

7. Take the new sales rep to lunch

8. Catch up on correspondence

9. Plan the company open day

10. Stocktake.

Now that you have your list of priorities, you can start working on the important tasks right away. Keep at it until they're done or until you're ready to compare a new set of tasks.

You can apply this prioritisation process to anything: the kind of car you're going to buy, the list of weekend jobs you're going to tackle, even the people you'll ask to your wedding. It will work like a charm.

A friendly reminder

The first step you take in carrying out a plan of action is often the most important one. It can help overcome the inertia that has held you back in the past, and it can lead you into a continuous pattern of growth and development.

A *leading task* (Step 7 – Implementation) is one that breaks the shackles of inertia and gets you involved immediately in satisfying a goal. It could be something as simple as sharpening your pencil before you begin a report. Or it could be looking up the addresses and phone numbers of the new clients you're going to call on.

Write down a leading task for each of the eight planning steps you're about to take, and before you know it, you'll be well on your way to reaching your goal.

Make your leading tasks relatively easy so you don't have to put a lot of effort into them. Just make sure that each task is pertinent to the long-term goals you're hoping to achieve.

A final word

When asked why he spent so much time in planning and thinking about the future, Charles Kettering, then chairman of General Motors, replied, 'My interest is in the future because I'm going to spend the rest of my life there.'

Your past is gone, your future lies ahead of you like ripening fruit. The time to take your first step is now. Don't let any more days get away without filling them to the brim with productive activities.

Recognise the power in planning and the promise it holds for controlling your future. Have the courage and commitment to start planning today. Do it now!

Further Reading from Kogan Page

Delegating for Results, Robert B Maddux

Effective Meeting Skills: How to Make Meetings More Productive, Marion E Haynes

Effective Performance Appraisals, Robert B Maddux*

Effective Presentation Skills, Steve Mandel

The Fifty-Minute Supervisor: A Guide for the Newly Promoted, Elwood N Chapman

How to Communicate Effectively, Bert Decker*

How to Develop a Positive Attitude, Elwood N Chapman*

How to Develop Assertiveness, Sam R Lloyd

How to Motivate People, Twyla Dell*

Make Every Minute Count: How to Manage Your Time Effectively, Marion E Haynes

Managing Disagreement Constructively, Herbert S Kindler

Managing Organisational Change, C Scott and D T Jaffe

Managing Quality Customer Service, William B Martin

Project Management, Marion E Haynes

Risk Taking, Herbert S Kindler

Successful Negotiation, Robert B Maddux

Team Building: An Exercise in Leadership, Robert B Maddux

*Also available on cassette